UP CLOSE

T. REX

PAUL HARRISON

Published in 2008 by Franklin Watts
Reprinted in 2010

Copyright © 2008 Arcturus Publishing Limited

Franklin Watts
338 Euston Road
London NW1 3BH

Franklin Watts Australia
Level 17/207 Kent Street
Sydney NSW 2000

Author: Paul Harrison
Designer (new edition): Silvie Rabbe
Editor (new edition): Fiona Tulloch

Picture credits: Ardea London Ltd: page 3, bottom right; page 6; page 8, bottom left; page 10, top right; page 14; page 15; Nature Picture Library: page 10, bottom left; Photolibrary (OSF): back cover and page 13, top right and bottom left; The Field Museum, Chicago: page 4, top right, N89671_53c: John Weinstein; The Natural History Museum: front cover; page 2; page 4, bottom left; page 5, top left; page 5, bottom right; page 7, top left; page 7, bottom right and page 8, top right; page 9; page 11; page 15; Science Photo Library: title page; page 3, top right; page 12; page 16.

A CIP catalogue record for this book is available from the British Library

Dewey number: 567.9' 129   568·19

ISBN: 978-1-4451-0135-4

SL000950EN

Printed in China

Franklin Watts is a division of Hachette Children's Books, an Hachette UK Company
www.hachette.co.uk

Contents

King of the

Millions of years before humans arrived, the world belonged to the dinosaurs. They ruled the earth for around 160 million years. Dinosaurs came in all shapes and sizes, but *Tyrannosaurus rex* (tie-RAN-o-SORE-us rex) stood out from the rest. What was T. rex really like? Was it as fearsome as we think? People are still trying to find the answers.

HUGE
Tyrannosaurus rex was one of the biggest *carnivores*, or meat-eating dinosaurs, ever discovered. It grew to 4.3 metres high and lived in North America around 85 to 65 million years ago.

Dinosaurs

The name Tyrannosaurus rex means "tyrant lizard king".

NO GRASS HERE

There was no grass during the time of Tyrannosaurus rex. There were some other familiar plants though, including figs, ferns, conifers and sycamores.

FOOD FACTS

Surprisingly, most dinosaurs were vegetarians! About 70 per cent were *herbivores*, or plant-eaters, and only 30 per cent were carnivores.

Rex Ruled the

Everyone knows that T. rex was among the most dangerous predators of its day. So how was it able to stay at the top of the *food chain* for thousands of years?

People who study dinosaurs are called palaeontologists.

END OF AN ERA

Tyrannosaurus rex was alive at the end of the reign of the dinosaurs. This was during the *Cretaceous period*. Scientists know most about this era.

World

BIG WORLD

In the Cretaceous world there were just two *continents* called Gondwana and Laurasia.

SCALY

T. rex had coarse, bumpy skin like an alligator. It would have felt like jagged stones.

Fearsome Find

There have been around thirty T. rex skeletons discovered in the world so far. An old, perfectly-preserved fossil attracts a lot of attention —and a lot of trouble.

SUE FOR KEEPS

Sue was discovered in 1990 in South Dakota, USA. A legal battle began about who owned the skeleton. In the end, the owner of the ranch where she was found was said to be the legal owner.

DETECTIVE

Scientists like Jack Horner are hunting for T. rex fossils.

FEMME FATALE

Sue is the largest and most complete skeleton of a Tyrannosaurus rex ever found. She is now in the Field Museum in Chicago, USA.

SECOND PRIZE

The team who discovered Sue didn't get to keep her, but they have the skeleton of a T. rex called Stan, who was found two years after Sue.

Sue was named after the woman who found her, Sue Hendrickson.

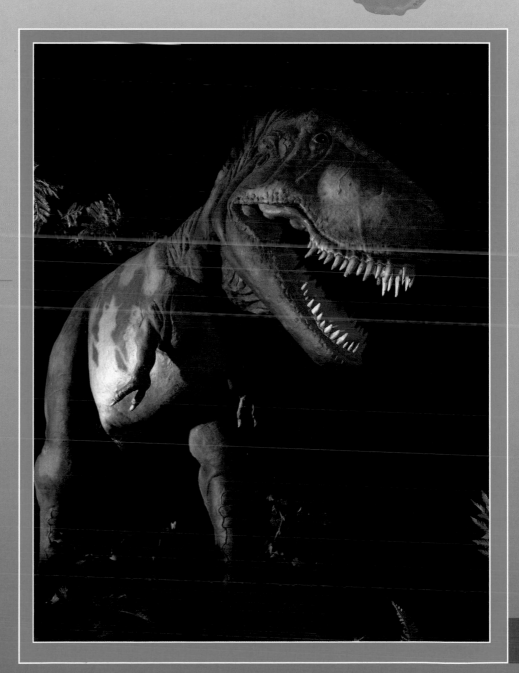

MOVING MONSTER

Visitors to London's Natural History Museum can get up close to a life-sized, *animatronic* model Tyrannosaur.

Straight to

T he huge size of the Tyrannosaur's head made it a terrifying dinosaur. Its mouth was packed full of scary, dangerous-looking teeth.

Tyrannosaurs were always growing new teeth to replace old or lost ones.

MOUTHFUL OF MISERY

The Tyrannosaur had sixty razor-sharp teeth. They measured up to 15 cm long and were curved.

the Point

BIG BITE

A T. rex's mouth was big enough to swallow a human whole and its teeth were strong enough to chomp through thick dinosaur bones.

SMALL ARMS

T. rex had very short, strong arms with two claws at the end. Scientists don't know what they were used for.

MEET THE NEIGHBOURS

Scientists believe that *Giganotosaurus* (gi-GAN-toe-SORE-us) and *Carcharodontosaurus* (car-CHA-row-DON-toe-SORE-us) might have been even bigger than T. rex.

Savage or

Everyone agrees that Tyrannosaurs were super-carnivores. However, palaeontologists can't agree on whether they hunted for their food or scavenged for it (eating animals that had already been killed).

HUNTER
T. rex's strong head would have been useful for attacking other dinosaurs to eat them.

NOSY
Scavengers, such as vultures, can smell *carrion* from great distances. T. rex also had a good sense of smell.

Scavenge?

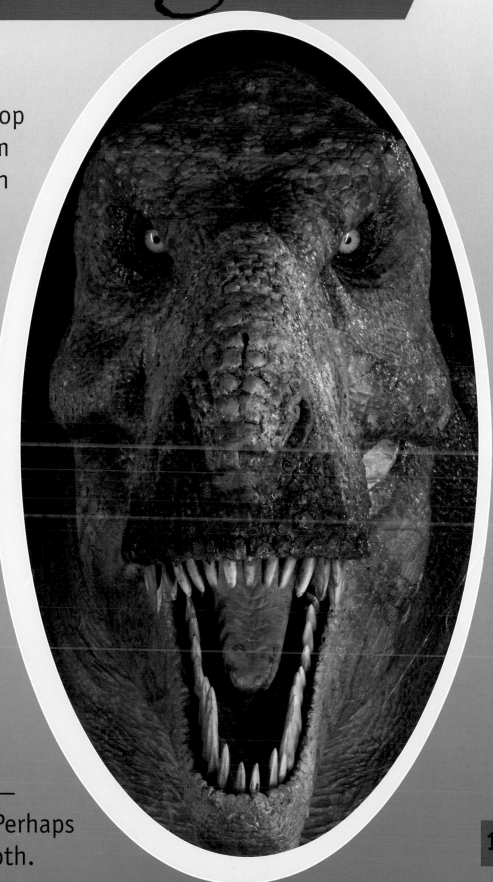

SLOWCOACH

Tyrannosaurs had a top speed of about 64 km per hour—faster than a human, but pretty slow compared to other dinosaurs.

EYE CAN SEE YOU

Tyrannosaurus had forward-facing eyes just like predators—such as tigers—do. Does this mean they were hunters?

OVER TO YOU

Hunter or scavenger— what do you think? Perhaps T. rex was a bit of both.

Dangerous

The Cretaceous forest was a dangerous place for a baby dinosaur. They could be crushed by large plant-eating dinosaurs or eaten by other carnivores. They could even be eaten by one of their parents!

Some people believe that all dinosaurs had feathers.

HATCHING OUT

Like all dinosaurs, Tyrannosaurus would have started life in an egg. Some scientitsts think they covered their eggs in earth or leaves, like crocodiles do today.

Start

PERFECT EGGS

The first fossilized dinosaur eggs were found in France in 1869. They were about the size and shape of footballs and contained over two litres of fluid! No one has found a T. rex egg yet, though.

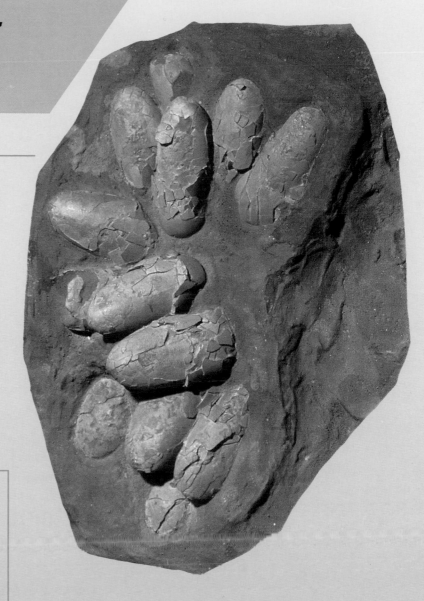

PARENT TROUBLE

Were Tyrannosaurs good parents? A mother Tyrannosaur would have looked after her young, but male Tyrannosaurs may have seen their babies as a threat, and may have tried to kill and eat them.

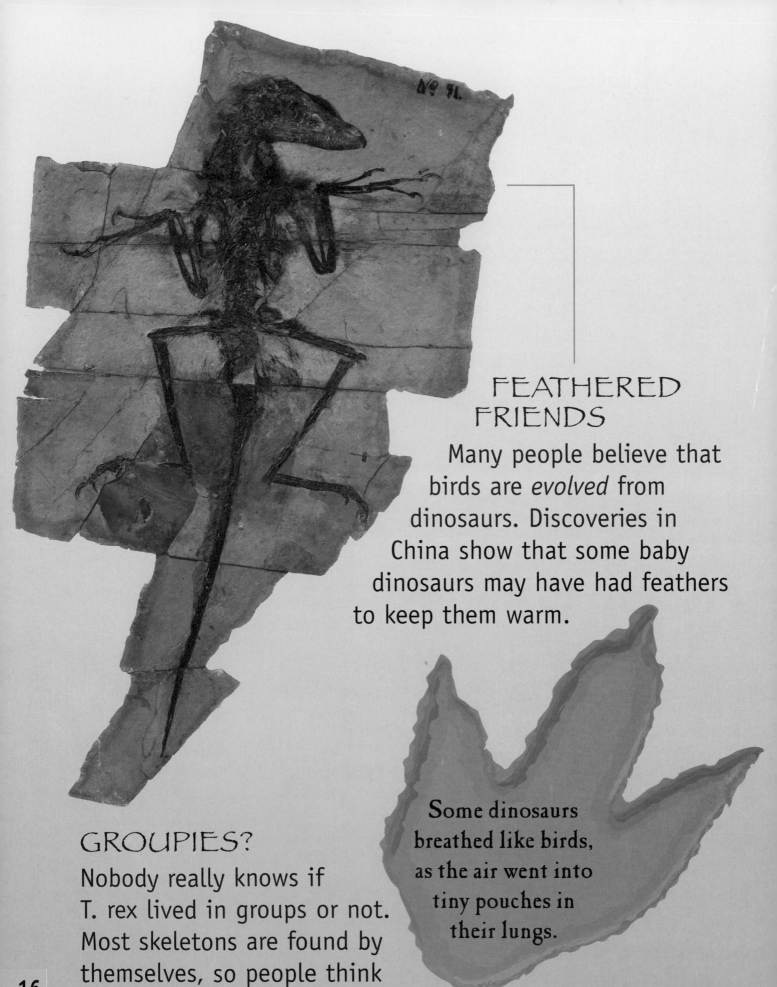

FEATHERED FRIENDS

Many people believe that birds are *evolved* from dinosaurs. Discoveries in China show that some baby dinosaurs may have had feathers to keep them warm.

Some dinosaurs breathed like birds, as the air went into tiny pouches in their lungs.

GROUPIES?

Nobody really knows if T. rex lived in groups or not. Most skeletons are found by themselves, so people think they lived on their own.

Going, Going, Gone

There are lots of theories about why dinosaurs disappeared. People believed that a huge *asteroid* hit the earth. Clouds of dust blocked out the sun's rays, and the earth grew cold. The dinosaurs couldn't cope with the colder weather and died. But is this the real story?

FADING OUT

Dinosaurs had been decreasing in number for millions of years because the earth's temperature was changing. They would have died off even without an asteroid hitting the earth.

17

HOLEY PROOF

A crater off the coast of Mexico exists which suggests that an asteroid really did hit the earth years ago. The hole is called the Chicxulub crater and it's off the Yucatán Peninsula of Mexico. It's under the sea, but we know it's over 179 km across.

SHOWER OF DESTRUCTION

After the huge asteroid hit the earth, the debris finally settled and formed a layer in the rocks. This is known as the K/T boundary and is found all over the world. Below this line you can find dinosaur fossils, but above the line there is nothing.

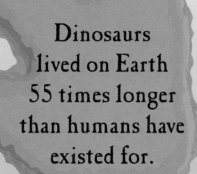

Dinosaurs lived on Earth 55 times longer than humans have existed for.

NO MORE PLANTS

Some people think that mammals may have eaten all the dinosaur eggs. Others say there wasn't enough for plant-eaters to eat so they died out—meaning the carnivores had nothing to eat either.

Everything we know about dinosaurs comes from the work of fossil-hunters, palaeontologists and other scientists. The newest technology is being used to try and find out even more.

HARD WORK

Preparing fossils takes a long time. It can take years to prepare a single fossil for display in a museum.

RAINBOW REX?

We can't tell what colour T. rex was. If it was a hunter, it would have been a neutral colour to blend into the background, like lions do.

Know?

The only way palaeontologists can find out more about dinosaurs is if more fossils are found.

—DIRTY JOB

Palaeontologists have to inspect dinosaur poo to discover what they ate. Fossilized poo is called coprolite.

WARM OR COLD?

Was T. rex warm- or cold-blooded? Dinosaurs were reptiles so they could have been cold-blooded. Scientists still don't know the answer.

21

Glossary

ANIMATRONICS
Technology used to create moving robot animals.

ASTEROID
One of many rocky objects, varying in size that circle the Sun.

CARNIVORE
A meat-eating animal.

CARRION
The dead or decaying flesh of an animal.

CONTINENT
A large area of land that contains lots of countries.

CRETACEOUS PERIOD
The period of time from 146 to 65 million years ago.

EVOLVE
To develop gradually from one thing into another.

FOOD CHAIN
A system where the smallest animal is eaten by a larger one, which in turn is eaten by an even bigger one, etc.

HERBIVORE
A plant-eating animal.

Further Reading

1001 Facts About Dinosaurs
Sue Grabham (Editor), DK Children, 1st
Edition, 2002

**Allosaurus And Other Jurassic Meat-
Eaters (Dinosaurs Of North America)**
Daniel Cohen, Capstone Press, 1995

Dinosaur (DK Experience)
John Malam, Dorling Kindersley
Publishers Ltd, 2006

Dinosaurs And Prehistoric Creatures
Michael Teitelbaum, Rourke Publishing,
1994

**Scholastic Dinosaurs A to Z:
The Ultimate Dinosaur Encyclopedia**
Don Lessem, New York NY: Scholastic,
2003

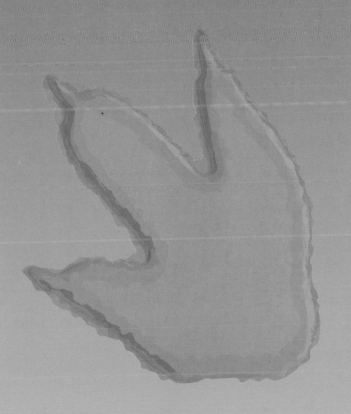

Index